D0948396

A FATHER

A Father

PUZZLE

SIBYLLE LACAN
TRANSLATED BY ADRIAN NATHAN WEST

THE MIT PRESS
CAMBRIDGE, MASSACHUSETTS
LONDON, ENGLAND

Originally published as *Un père: Puzzle* © Editions GALLIMARD, Paris, 1994.

This book was set in Arnhem Pro by The MIT Press. Printed and bound in the United States of America.

Library of Congress Cataloging-in-Publication Data

Names: Lacan, Sibylle, author. | West, Adrian Nathan, translator. |
   Translation of: Lacan, Sibylle. Pere.
Title: A father : puzzle / Sibylle Lacan ; translated by Adrian Nathan West.
Other titles: Pere. English
Description: Cambridge, MA : The MIT Press, 2019.
Identifiers: LCCN 2018019330 | ISBN 9780262039314 (hardcover : alk. paper)
Subjects: LCSH: Lacan, Jacques, 1901–1981. | Lacan, Sibylle.
Classification: LCC BF109.L23 L2313 2019 | DDC 150.19/5092 [B]—dc23 LC
   record available at https://lccn.loc.gov/2018019330

10   9   8   7   6   5   4   3   2   1

TO ALL THOSE WHO BELIEVED IN ME

CONTENTS

NOTICE

This book is not a novel or an embellished autobiography. It contains not an ounce of fiction. No invented detail has been placed herein with the aim of making the story more alluring or padding out the text. My purpose has been another: to let rise to the surface of my memory everything significant, everything intense—be it tragic or comic—that occurred between my father and me. To speak not of the man in general, and even less of the psychoanalyst, but of the father Jacques Lacan was to me. It is a purely subjective work, based on my recollections of the time and a vision of events that I have arrived at today.

I wrote the first page one night in August 1991, in one go. It is thus, in a certain sense, the most perfect. All my life, I have written this way, spontaneously, impulsively, and without subsequent editing. For me, this was a matter of principle. Unfortunately, this is only possible with extremely short texts, and in the present case, I have had to rework a great deal: to correct, to look for the right word, to refine the story as much as possible. Not to mention the exhausting effort of remembering.

The subtitle *puzzle* alludes to the fact that I did not write this text in a consistent manner. In the midst of disorder, I have written what I would call "bursts," or rather, I have followed their imperious unveiling in my memory, resolved—because to do otherwise would have been impossible—not to arrange them until the end. I have written, so to speak, blindly, without any precise design, whether in the formal sense, or as forethought; without knowing which scene, which image, I would wind up with once the bursts, the morsels, the pieces were assembled.

In any case, I should like to offer the uninitiated reader a rough outline of my family topography. Blondin is my mother's maiden name, which she would reclaim when she divorced my father. Maman was the first wife of Jacques Lacan, my father. She had three children by him: Caroline, Thibaut, and me. Bataille is the name of my father's second wife. They had a daughter together, Judith, who retained the family name Bataille because her parents had not yet divorced their respective spouses when she came into the world. Miller is the name Judith would take after her marriage to Jacques-Alain Miller.

As far as places go, I believe the text makes clear that Rue Jadin is where my sister, my brother, and I lived with our mother until we moved away on reaching adulthood. Regarding Rue de Lille, who doesn't now know that Doctor Lacan's offices were located at 5 Rue de Lille in Paris?

A Father

When I was born, my father was already no longer there. I could even say that when I was conceived, he was already elsewhere, he no longer really lived with my mother. A meeting in the country between husband and wife, after everything was already over, marks the origin of my birth. I am the fruit of despair; some will say of desire, but I do not believe them.

Why then do I feel the need to speak of my father now, when it is my mother whom I loved and continue to love after her death, after *their* deaths?

Affirmation of my heritage, snobbery—I am the daughter of Lacan—or a vindication of the Blondin-Lacan clan against the Bataille-Millers?

Whichever it may be, my sister, now gone, my older brother, and I are the only ones who bear the name Lacan. And that is what this is all about.

In my memory, I didn't know my father until after the war (I was born at the end of 1940). I don't know if this is really true, I never questioned Maman about the subject. Probably he used to "pass through" now and then. But in my reality, there was Maman, and that was all. Not that anything was missing; things had never been otherwise. We knew we had a father, but apparently a father was something that wasn't there. For us, Maman was everything: love, security, authority.

An image of the period remains fixed in my memory, as though frozen in a photograph: my father's silhouette in the doorway, one Thursday when he'd come to see us: immense, swathed in a vast overcoat, there he was, looking burdened by who knows what worry. A custom was established: he would come to Rue Jadin once a week for lunch.

He spoke formally to my mother and addressed her as "my dear." Maman, when she spoke of him, called him "Lacan."

She had advised us, at the beginning of the school year, when we had to fill out the ritual questionnaire, to write the word "Doctor" in the blank asking for father's profession. In those days, psychoanalysis was seen as little more than charlatanism.

It was on the island of Noirmoutier, where we would regularly spend our long vacation, that "the abnormal" glided into our lives. Our young, well-intentioned friends revealed to us that our parents were divorced and that, and as a result, Maman would be sent to hell (!). I don't know which of these two disclosures hit me harder. At naptime, my brother and I held a long consultation.

The years continued to unwind. Maman played every role. We were "handsome," intelligent, and worked hard in class. She was proud of us, but she wanted us to grow up. After the war, that was her obsession: guiding the three of us into adulthood.

Papa, for our birthdays, would give us superb gifts (I believe it took me far too long to understand that he was not the one who picked them out).

In a timeless time, in an indeterminate space—though I did learn from my brother, some years back, that it was not something I merely dreamt—an extraordinary event took place. Childhood, Brittany, Thibaut, my father, and I. What were we doing there with my father? Where was my mother? Why was Caroline—in my recollection—not there? The three of us were visiting a castle. Thibaut was racing down the spiral stairway of a tower. Where am I, exactly, with respect to him? And my father? *But I see this*: at a bend, to the right, is an opening that gives directly onto the emptiness, a door without a ledge or parapet. Thibaut, in his boyish eagerness, barrels toward it. My father catches him by his clothes. A miracle!

Second scene: we rejoin Maman and I tell her, upset, how Thibaut has skirted death. No shouting, no weeping, no apparent emotion. I do not understand. I have never understood. My brother has retained no tragic memory of this event. My father never spoke of it again. Maman, who did not react at the time, never again brought up the disaster we had only just avoided.

Formentera is the name of the island I have chosen as a second home, as a vacation home: FORT M'ENTERRA.*

*"Fort/the strong one buried me."

The law of primogeniture governed life at home. In this way, Maman reproduced what she had experienced in childhood—she was, like me, the youngest—and what she considered "normal," inevitable, in other words: just the way things were. Above us all was Caroline, four years older than I (though the distance seemed far greater). She held all the power ... and all the privileges. She became a woman very early on, tall, with long, thick hair of a blond color unusual in our region, flourishing like a Renoir (I was always the smallest in my class, a blend of femininity and failed boyishness), *beautiful* in the eyes of all (I was only ever "cute"), remarkably gifted and intelligent (first prize all her life, head of the class, a brilliant university career— I was a good student, but always had to work for it); in a word, a goddess incarnate, she lived in a world apart, closer to that of Maman than to ours. By "ours" I mean my brother's and mine, who were, throughout our entire childhood, "the little ones." And yet, there was still another subdivision in force: Thibaut was not only a year older than I, but also a boy—an incontestable advantage in the eyes of Maman, despite her professed ideas about the equality of the sexes. And so it was natural that he not make his bed, that he not set the table, and other "details" that clashed profoundly with my sense of justice.

If it happened that my brother and I joined forces against my sister, who did not hesitate, in the most extreme cases, to defend her privileges with force, the result, most often—the general character of these occasions, if I may put it this way—was the exposure of my own inferiority. I was described—of course, it was only a "wisecrack," and even Maman laughed along—as "dumb, ugly, and nasty." Another of their mottos was "Sibylle is anything but a thief" (!). Naturally all that might have been funny had the "victim" not always been the same, or if the occasional compliment, or some gesture of tenderness, had sometimes come afterward, to compensate for that mania for belittling me. Even if she saw I was right, Maman would never step in during arguments, to avoid offending the older ones—but things were different when I was found to be at fault.

Perhaps the constant oppression I endured at my brother's and sister's hands explains my passion for justice and my outrage in the face of humiliation—good things in themselves—but what about my outsized need for attention and my extreme sensitivity, verging on frailty?

My father went further in his diagnosis: watching that cruel and hurtful game play out one day with bewilderment, he intervened in my favor, and addressing Thibaut and Caroline, concluded: "You'll end up turning her into an idiot."

And if a father was good for anything, it was that: to administer justice ...

I saw my father one on one when we had dinner together. He would take me to fancy restaurants where I had the chance to taste expensive dishes: oysters, lobster, sumptuous desserts—the height of indulgence, in my eyes, was meringue glacée. But most importantly, I was with my father and I felt good. He was attentive, loving, "respectful." At last, I was a person in my own right. Our conversation was interspersed with peaceful silences, and sometimes I would reach across the table and take his hand. He never talked to me about his private life, and I never questioned him on the subject, nor did it even cross my mind. He would show up out of nowhere and it never surprised me in the least. The essential thing: *he was there*, and I was "flushed, enraptured," as the poet said.

I *see* myself, a teenager, as if frozen in time, having lunch at the family table and proclaiming, before I'd sat down (no one had asked me): "I will never marry."

An exemplary avowal (in light of the place accorded me at the aforementioned table), but still, I have never been able to recall what it was that provoked this *cri du coeur*, this public declaration, this paving stone hurled into the tranquil waters of an ordinary meal partaken in by an (almost) ordinary family.

Soon after I was born (or was Maman still pregnant with me?), my father elatedly announced to my mother, with juvenile malice, that he had a child on the way. I don't know how my mother felt or what words she uttered: did she make a show of her suffering, did she reproach him, did she fly into a rage, or was she firm and dignified, keeping to herself that inward disintegration, the shock of the mortal blow, the death that crept into her soul? The one thing I do know, because Maman told me, is that my father said to her, when he had finished talking: "I'll make it up to you a hundred times over" (!).

My mother, an upright, faithful woman, was alone with three small children when the war came, along with the occupiers, and there loomed a period of worldwide horror whose end was impossible to foresee.

When I was born, Maman hardly looked after me, she hadn't wanted me and she was elsewhere, sunken in her own personal abyss. Can I blame her? But I do think my entire life was marked by that emergence into the world in emotional solitude.

A year after my birth, the divorce was finalized, at my mother's behest.

It was on the occasion of my older sister's marriage—I was seventeen years old at the time—that I learned of the existence of Judith, less than a year my junior. Maman had hidden her from us because, as she explained, our father was not "married." Things were like that then. But other rancors, other sufferings must also have encouraged her silence. My father said that Judith wanted to, ought to, attend her sister's marriage. Maman gave in.

The news shook me. I had another sister, and I was anxious to get to know her.

The future held many disappointments in store for me ...

My first real meeting with Judith crushed me. She was so pleasant, so perfect, and I so awkward and bungling. She was all sociability and poise, I was the Peasant of the Danube. She had a womanly air, I still looked like a child. This feeling lasted a long time. Later, I would come across her type again and would know how to react. But at the time, I was overwhelmed, ashamed. Moreover, she was studying philosophy and I was *only* studying languages. How many times did she cross my path at the Sorbonne and pretend not to recognize me? I was mortified, I didn't have the presence of mind to call her out. Twice I spent vacation with my father. The first time in Saint-Tropez, the second in Italy, on the seaside, I no longer remember where. Judith was in Saint-Tropez, too. She made me feel the whole of my mediocrity. A hallucinated memory is the sight of my father and Judith, dancing like two lovers at a village fair in Ramatuelle. What world had I plunged into? Was a father not a father? She joined us in Italy after a trip to Greece with colleagues from the department, all of them apparently in love with her. Many were rejected in Athens; only the chosen ones remained till the end. This story made my father very proud. No disclosures to me. She was Queen. Had I been to Greece? Did I have admirers? That summer, for the first time, I fell mysteriously ill: a general enervation, no more longing, no more pleasure, a dreadful turmoil. To reassure myself, I blamed the heat. When I returned to Paris, everything fell back into place.

When we were sixteen, eighteen (?), Maman asked my brother and me if we wanted to take the name Blondin. Instinctively, we said no.

In April 1962—I was twenty-one years old—I fell ill. Everything pointed to the flu and I was treated accordingly. I remained in bed for around a week, then the fever broke and they said I was better. But the other symptoms persisted: an immense fatigue, both physical—I needed twelve hours of sleep per day—and intellectual: I struggled to keep up in class and had even greater difficulties with memorization. From the time I woke up to the time I lay down, I had an unbearable foggy feeling. I couldn't read. Even movies left me stupefied. In short, I had no energy at all. All I had left was the will to recover. I was convinced I had something. I saw many doctors—generalists and specialists—and suffered through many examinations. They never found anything. Drawing on what I'd already learned, I managed to finish my studies, like a sleepwalker.

I was supposed to leave for Moscow for a year in December, to perfect my Russian but also to enjoy a transition year, a sort of vacation before entering the workforce. This project meant a great deal to me, and my distress grew as the months passed and I feared I wouldn't be able to go.

As I remember, it was Maman who had the idea of calling on my father to help. The appointment on Rue Jadin was set for such-and-such an hour on such-and-such a day. I had great expectations for that meeting. If all the stupid doctors hadn't been able to cure me, who but my father—the eminent psychoanalyst, whose genius I had never once doubted—could understand me, save me? The situation was all the more nightmarish because those around me, understanding nothing of my illnesses and afflictions, seemed to suspect me of malingering, of laziness, even—why not?— of faking it.

I *see* myself on the balcony at the appointed hour, looking out for my father to arrive. Time passed, he still wasn't there. My impatience grew. How could he be so late, given the circumstances?

Rue Jadin is so short you can take it all in with one glance. A few yards from our building was a house of assignation, discreet, frequented by people with "class." From my lookout, I suddenly saw a woman emerge from it with brisk steps. A few seconds later, a man departed in turn. Dumbfounded, I recognized my father.

How could he have tormented me so just to satisfy his own desires *first*? How dare he fuck a woman on Rue Jadin, steps away from the home of his children and his ex-wife? I went back inside, seething with indignation.

The rest of the story? My memories are hazy, and with good reason. All I have retained of my father's words to me that day is this: a separation from my mother would do me the utmost good, and I should leave without hesitation. I was stunned. What could Maman have to do with the dreadful state I was in? What did he even know about my relationship with Maman? Throughout my childhood and adolescence, I had always been independent, spending most of my time with friends my own age, and I barely understood the fundamental role the existence, the presence of a mother played. From a young age, I would leave Maman for vacation without a care, as most children do, absorbed in the pleasures that awaited me. (But then, I remember, our reunions at the train station always moved me deeply. I would see her in the distance walking up the platform, tall, blonde, and slender, alert, and her expression, her gait communicated the love of a mother finally able to hold her child in her arms again.)

So the whole blessed family now pushed me to go— my father, my uncle on my mother's side, who was a hospital surgeon, a neurologist cousin, a close friend of my uncle, an eminent doctor who had examined me, even my mother—and I left, as scheduled, on December 18, 1962, determined to say nothing to anyone for a year, come what may. I began keeping a journal on the very train that would take me to the other end of Europe, feeling that for me, this was the only way not to founder: to write, now that I could no longer read, to fix the days, now that memory had failed me, to trap the words before they fled, to find a reflection, a proof of my existence on sheets of paper, on pages scribbled over without concern for their beauty. To try to survive, nothing more.

When I returned from the USSR at the beginning of 1964, my condition was unchanged. As I'd promised myself, I hadn't breathed a word of my sufferings, and curiously, no one noticed anything. At the French embassy where I worked, I had managed to fool everyone, because my job was below my abilities and my education. The people I met, whether Russian or French, seemed to find all sorts of virtues in me—never had I felt so flattered—and I even passed for "amusing," as witnessed by a passage in my journal I came upon several years ago where I'd recorded, with astonishment, a Russian friend's remark about me: *kakaya vesselaya!** Every week, for a year, I sent my mother a letter via diplomatic post and told her everything I thought might interest or amuse her, never once alluding to my illnesses. Perhaps Maman believed I was "cured." I should add that normally I would have made great progress in Russian, with the solid base I had acquired at the École des langues orientales, my talent for living languages in general, and above all, the fact that, outside of working hours, I was immersed in Russian life. But instead I got nowhere, and I have always regretted that. I managed just enough to

---

*"What fun!"

understand and make myself understood, not without difficulty; my memory betrayed me, and I was far from speaking fluent Russian when my stay there was at an end.

But let's return to Paris in that January of 1964. Feeling unable to work, I decided to go back to university to buy a bit more time and put my intellectual capacities to the test. With those close to me, I had avoided the issue of my health, hoping to make a final effort, to try for one last time to get over it on my own. I soon had to give up. Impossible to study, to learn, to recall. Always the same weariness, that foggy sensation, the same absence of emotion. My life was hell.

Eventually I confessed everything: distress on my mother's part, sniggering from my brother, an sos call to my father. I demanded a sleep cure—not knowing exactly what that was—my obsession: to sleep as long as possible and wake up rested ... and healed. My father took my request to heart and told me he would "make inquiries." When the inquiries had been made, he informed me that sleep cures created dependency and were therefore best avoided (looking back, I have often wondered why my father, a trained psychiatrist, had needed to investigate the subject, but let's move on). Then and only then did he propose I undergo analysis. "I can't treat you," he felt obliged to explain (as if I were so ignorant that I didn't know that), "but I can find someone for you."

He sent me to Madame A. I saw her for around a year, nothing happened, the metro ride exhausted me. I quit. Some time passed, I reiterated my plea. He chose another analyst for me: Madame P., and I went to her for several years. Even before her, I had met the person who would be my first lover, and thanks to whom I began a slow recovery: he was the first person who listened to me and *believed* me without trying to understand, without even once casting doubt on my words, he loved me as I was, passionately. (Here, across time and space, I would like to express to him my gratitude.)

Madame P. was a gentle and well-meaning woman, and I do not think the work I did with her was pointless. Unfortunately, as the years passed, the clues piled up, and one day I became convinced she was my father's mistress. I left her immediately.

Several months later, a friend alluded to their affair in front of me, and I realized that everyone who was anyone in Parisian psychoanalysis had known about it, except for me.

(I chose my third analyst *myself*, demanding he keep it a secret.)

When I asked my father about my "illness" some two years after its onset ("What do I have, then?"), he responded: in the nineteenth century, we would called you *neurasthenic*.

(Another person, whose name I will not mention, speaks of "melancholy," and claims that one never recovers from it. My analyst did not agree with the latter point.)

Before I started to work, in the proper sense, and not without difficulty—in other words, before 1975—I would occasionally "consult" my father when I had doubts about the origins of my malady, with its purely physical symptoms of perpetual fatigue, an excessive need for sleep, the discrepancy between the norm and the hours I kept in my own daily life, etc. His attitude varied. Most of the time, he would say something like, "How's your analysis going?" That would leave me sad and perplexed. But on occasion, when I managed to convince him of the unbearable, insurmountable, and immutable nature of my pains, he would send me to a general practitioner, strongly suggesting I tell him not to overstep the boundaries of *his* specialty. He wanted the doctor to behave as a doctor, and not stray into psychological considerations.

I should add that, after I asked him one day if I might be suffering from an organic disorder of the brain, he replied that if that were case, we would have known by now, with an implicit allusion to the gruesome evolution of syndromes of that sort. I don't know whether I was more bewildered or terrified.

I was in my thirties. It was a time when I didn't work, was incapable of work. A time of emptiness and pain. The days of Montparnasse, of wandering. When I was at the Select, an old acquaintance—a young man who has since become a psychoanalyst himself—saw me and came over. He had interesting news to tell me. Do you know, he said to me, that in his *Who's Who* listing, your father has only one daughter, Judith? In my head, everything went black. The rage only came afterward.

(Some days later, I felt the need to confirm this for myself at the publisher: the-friend-who-wished-me-well had not been mistaken.)

I hated my father for several years. How could it have been otherwise? Did he not abandon *all* of us—Maman, my sister, my brother, and me—with the torments his absence had left in its wake? Only Caroline seemed to have emerged unharmed—at least, to an outside observer; she never confided in me. Note that Caroline was the only one to have had a father and a mother in her early childhood. The foundations had been laid ...

That resentment, that fury, appeared relatively late in my analysis. I took my time in rebelling. I judged him guilty of the family disaster I became conscious of little by little, and of my own breakdown at the end of my adolescence. I am aware of the importance he attached to the "discourse of the mother," but why should Maman have trumped things up? Besides, she never told us anything concrete, never tried to turn us against him. The facts spoke for themselves. He never took care of us and was gone during the first years of Thibaut's life and mine. Maman was the one who raised us, who loved us from one day to the next. My father lived his life, his work, and to us, our own lives seemed like an accident in his story, something from his past that he couldn't quite ignore. I know he loved us, in his way. He was an intermittent father, a father in fragments. I also know he was aware of his failings toward us, as the following anecdote shows.

One evening when I went to meet him in the Rue de Lille for dinner, I found him in the company of his manicurist, who was exercising her trade. He introduced me to her with pride. The young woman addressed me and began: "So, your father ..."

"Barely," my father interrupted her with a sigh.

As usual, I made an appointment one day to see my father at dinnertime. It's urgent, I told Gloria, his faithful secretary. Why was I in such a rush to talk to him? I no longer remember.

I was still living in the Rue Jadin, this was after Russia, I would have been twenty-three or twenty-four. My father came by car to pick me up, as he used to do at the time. From the sidewalk, he yelled at me, furious: "I hope you're not going to tell me you're marrying some imbecile!"

"A father, barely," but a father all the same. He was systematically mistrustful of everyone I loved. If I was foolish enough to mention someone to him, he would ask me right away: "Who is that?" (Incomprehension on my part.) *"What's his name?"* As though my "boyfriends" were celebrities, or their names (however unknown they were) would tell him something about them. Naming them was especially painful for me; I felt like an informer, like a prisoner under interrogation. But if I tried to evade him, to convince him he would get nowhere, he would press me, and I would eventually bend to his will. For my father to wrest from me the name of the man I loved before I had shown any desire to speak of him seemed to me the height of indiscretion. And giving in to his insistence, the height of cowardice.

When I was a girl, I went to spend the weekend at my father's country house in Guitrancourt. I often took a bedroom on the same floor as he, but on the other side of the stairway, at the end of a short hallway—the main reason being that this room, apart from being pleasant, with a view onto the garden, had its own private bathroom.

It was a pleasure to wash up there because it was spacious and bright, with the slightly passé charm of provincial houses that accorded with my sense of the beautiful.

Late one morning, I was standing in the bathroom running a washcloth over my body. Suddenly (there was no lock) I heard the door open. I turned around trembling, my father was there in the doorway. He paused, said a tranquil "Excuse me, darling," and left just as calmly, closing the door behind him.

Just a glance, but it was enough ...

(I was FURIOUS.)

Maman had to go back to work after finding herself on her own. For a long time, she worked as an anesthesiologist alongside her brother. Later, when they began requiring a degree for this profession, she searched desperately for another job. For a while she designed patterns for scarves or drew advertisements (as a young girl, she was passionately devoted to painting), but her "manner" was unsuited to the tenor of the times, and she had to give it up. In the same way, she had to give up her position as a saleswoman in a modest boutique after only a few days: commerce inspired a phobia in her. Soon she gave up trying. Maman was no longer young, and I sensed she found this humiliating. From then on, she had to make do with my father's alimony payments, which were meager and rarely rose with the cost of living. This was a bit of "forgetfulness" on my father's part, and, since mother was not the sort to go begging, over time, her income remained flat. And yet we were still living at home, my brother and I—Caroline had already married, or else was on the verge of doing so.

And so we got by with the strictest economy—this proved an excellent education for us "children," but it was a risky and far from amusing exercise for a mature woman for whom the barest necessities, little by little, became unjustifiable luxuries.

Years later, when I had left Rue Jadin for the last time, I was tempted to bring up this matter of money with Maman, and I asked her flat out how much Papa gave her every month: it was a negligible sum, and since he owed her, I pressed her to make him give her more. Maman refused brusquely. That was beneath her. I saw my father often in those days and decided, on my own initiative, to broach the subject with him. The result was an outright success: he immediately doubled Maman's payment.

(Later, I tried again to have the amount brought up to date—in vain. My father was getting old, and with the years, his irrational attachment to money grew more pronounced.)

As far back as I can remember, I always saw, in my father's consulting room, presiding over the fireplace, a large photograph of Judith. This very beautiful black-and-white photo showed Judith as a girl, seated, discreetly dressed—a sweater and a pencil skirt—her long, straight black hair combed back, revealing her forehead.

What struck me immediately on entering the consulting room for the first time was her resemblance to Papa. Like him, she had an oval face, black hair, and a long nose (my own hair is light brown, my nose stubby, my face triangular, my cheekbones prominent). What I noticed afterward was her beauty, the intelligence of her expression, the elegance of her posture.

There was no other photo in the room.

To his patients, to us, to me, for over twenty years, my father seemed to be saying: Here is my daughter, my only daughter, here is my darling daughter.

It was in 1963, during my stay in Russia, that someone asked for the first time if I was related to Jacques Lacan. (I still remember the secretary at the embassy who posed this question to me.)

Why take note of what is probably no more than a trifle? To stress that never, during my childhood or adolescence, at school or university, was I "the daughter of." And I think that was a good thing—a blessing, a liberation.

In my adulthood, after my return from the USSR, the question grew more and more common, and my reaction, like my feelings, was muted. Did I really want to be Lacan's daughter? Was I proud of it, or irritated? Was there some fortune in being, *in certain people's eyes*, merely "the daughter of," in other words, no one?

The years passed and, with the help of my analyst, my feelings toward my father became clearer, more peaceful. I came to recognize him fully as my father. But above all—and this is even more important— today *I have faith in myself* and it matters little who my father is. Besides, if you think about it, are you not always your parents' daughter (or son)?

One evening—long after I'd reached adulthood—I had dinner with my father in a restaurant. As always, this was a special moment for me, but I confess I don't remember the details of that evening today. (Was it especially touching, especially warm?) What happened later, on the other hand, I have never forgotten.

I drove my father back to Rue de Lille in my little Austin, and when it was time for us to part, he said to me: "Watch out for yourself, darling, and please call me when you get home." He insisted. I was stunned. I had lived on my own, had always gone about alone, traveled alone—even to the very ends of the earth—without his showing the least worry, and suddenly I had before me a *fretful father* pleading for me to reassure him after a run-of-the-mill trip through Paris. I played along and promised I would phone him as soon as I got back.

Once home, I complied straightaway, afraid of waking him if I let even another minute pass: "Who is this? What? What's happened?" He was taken aback. I had to remind him of what he had asked of me.

When I hung up, I said to myself I had a true eccentric for a father, a bit *zinzin*, to use the term that was so dear to him.

The flowers ... My father gave me flowers on solemn occasions, imbued with gravity, laden with possible dangers. And yet the scenes I have held intact in my memory are linked for me with an irresistibly comic feeling.

As I said before, I left for Moscow in December 1962, to work for the French embassy for a full year: four seasons. It was agreed I would take the train—less expensive than an airplane—and I prepared to cross Europe, bypassing East Germany, in accordance with a directive from the Quai d'Orsay (at the time, ministries in the West saw this as a means of protesting the construction of the Berlin Wall).

It was my first long voyage (three days and three nights by train) and my first long separation from my family, my friends, my country. Moreover, I was crossing the Iron Curtain, and at a crucial moment in the Cold War (the Cuban Missile Crisis had just ended). (But the most important thing for me, the cruelest—and the very thing no one talked about—was that I was leaving with sickness in every part of my being, even in my mind: Would I be able to cope with my problems in that totalitarian country? Could my imprudence land me in prison? Would I be able to do the work expected of me?)

There I was on the station platform chatting with Maman before stowing my baggage in my compartment (some days before, I had reserved space for two suitcases and a trunk, because, they had warned me, you had to take everything with you). The departure time approached. Still nothing from my father. But no, there he was in the distance, hurrying toward us, panting. But what did he have in his hands? A parting gift, of course: a big clear plastic box with a sumptuous orchid inside. I loathe orchids, those pretentious and mortifying high-priced flowers. But what did it matter, my father had no reason to know that, the question was: what would I do with this awkward, fragile object for seventy-two hours, especially when I changed trains at the Soviet border? Astonished once again at my father's eccentricity, I nonetheless thanked him profusely.

It must be said, in the end, the thing made two people happy: at a way station in Poland, a young man sat in my compartment. His fiancée was waiting for him at the next stop. Far more than we, the Slavic people have kept alive the custom of giving flowers. Delighted, I seized the opportunity and handed him the orchid, which in this way fulfilled its proper mission.

The second "flower episode" took place a few years later, in 1969, when I had to undergo an emergency operation, a very traumatic one for a young woman, the seriousness of which was impossible to know in advance: they would have to "open me up" first and see. To be brief—though there were other disturbing aspects (the pain, the possible aftereffects)—what I naturally wished to know was: would I still be able to have children? My father came to see me on the eve of my operation, which would take place the very next morning, and I have to say his demeanor was a far cry from that of my uncle, the surgeon, who had treated me rather rudely during the days I spent under observation in his unit. Without mincing words, he told me, with great tenderness and gravity: "My darling, I promise you, you will know the entire truth."

But I am straying from my subject: the flowers. The day after my operation (the sympathetic reader will be glad to know that only my left ovary and fallopian tube were removed), at around four in the afternoon, there was a knock at the door to my room. "Come in," I said. Then there appeared, through the opening door, a gigantic flowerpot, I would say almost a whole bed's worth of flowers, in an enormous earthenware vessel, and behind it, my father, very small, holding onto it as if handling the blessed sacrament. A mad longing to laugh.

We exchanged the usual words between patient and visitor (I had never suffered so much in my life), then my father knelt at the foot of the bed and remained there for a long time in that posture, so strange for a nonbeliever.

As he stayed there, immobile, pensive, eyes closed, I thought, still laughing to myself: he's preparing his seminar.

My father was no athlete, to say the least (it was Maman who taught him to ride a bicycle when he was already past thirty). But with age he acquired a taste for action, with all the risks that such enthusiasm can bring with it in later life.

My first memory of this was his telling us one Thursday, to general hilarity, of his first foray into skiing, one so sensational he had immediately broken a leg. "You should have seen me, dear," he said to Maman with a childish pride and naivety, "people's jaws dropped when they watched me pass by ..."

I was able to admire his swimming skills with my own eyes the summer we spent in Italy. Stretched out on the sand beneath the sun, absorbed in the reading of some learned work, Papa got up all of a sudden in his flamboyant, emerald green swimsuit, ran toward the water with long strides, and, getting his upper body into the right position—arms outstretched, hands together (see *The Fenouillard Family*)—plunged into the sea with a loud splash. Then he breaststroked vigorously out into the open sea ... not far.

Another time, when we'd met for dinner, he told me he had crossed all of Paris on foot without the least fatigue, and concluded that the capital was nothing more than a village. I was speechless, for I had only ever seen my father walk with slow steps, visibly distracted, generally with his eyes turned toward his shoes, and I couldn't imagine him taking pleasure in such an exercise.

Finally, I will mention a scene that deeply wounded my leftist convictions. Once, when he was leaving our apartment, he found his car stuck between two other vehicles. Calling out to some unfortunate men passing by, he wrangled them into lifting up his car, while he made not the slightest gesture to help, instead standing to the side and giving orders. He did everything short of congratulating them with a "thank you kindly, my good men."

More than once, my father's behavior with others made me uncomfortable. The example of my mother, who treated everyone with the same kindness and respect, combined with my own conception of human beings as fellow creatures detached from any *hierarchy* related to birth or social position, explains why my father's attitude often shocked me.

If they didn't *resist*, if they let themselves be pushed around, "underlings" could expect the worst ... unless my father, whose moods were unpredictable, felt like playing the charmer just then.

Others before me have related with skill—and sometimes with indulgence—his conduct with Paquita, the old housekeeper from Spain who in later years replaced Gloria in his office after a certain hour. The poor thing was in such disarray, she looked like a spinning top, first twirling this way, then that, according to her employer's contradictory commands. It was painful to watch, and it made me ashamed for my father.

(A taxi driver, on the other hand, didn't hesitate to throw us out of his car one night on the *very first* street corner, that was how hateful my father had been to him before we'd even gotten rolling.)

But I will retell here an incident that brought me great suffering at the time (especially as I was deeply involved in it) and which, despite everything, I can't help but smile about today, given its frankly Ubu-esque character. In those days, I dabbled in leftist circles. My father took me to a famous restaurant. We went through the door, bowing and scraping from the headwaiter, too bad for him. He fawned over the "docteur" and mademoiselle his daughter. We took a table at a booth. Semidarkness. Upscale ambience, very snazzy. My father, menu in hand, sang the virtues of the cocoa-dusted truffle. Skeptical at first, I let myself be convinced. The truffle arrives. The headwaiter waits, bowing slightly. Under the two men's anxious gazes, I put the first bite in my mouth ... and then the catastrophe occurs. My father grills me with his booming voice: "Is it good? Is it good? If not, we'll leave, you know." Tense smile from the headwaiter. The doctor's daughter finds it insipid but puts herself resolutely on the side of the "people," the oppressed, the humiliated, and replies, as calmly as she can, "It's excellent."

That's how my father was.

I always admired my father's aptitude for self-absorption. The world around him might turn upside down, but if he was working, nothing could disturb him or distract him from his thoughts.

During the holiday in Italy I have already mentioned, he chose the main room in the villa as his work space. It was impossible to avoid him when going from one room to the other, leaving or coming in. I see my father seated at a large table, laden with books and papers, immobile, absent, while the family members in their skimpy clothes never stop passing by.

One afternoon, we went out to sea. A fisherman took us in a boat with a little motor. The view was magnificent: the vertiginous cliffs, the deep blue of the Mediterranean, the shimmer of light over water, the radiance of the sun, all of it was exhilarating. My father never looked up from his Plato. (The fisherman, from time to time, shot him a perturbed glance.)

In Guitrancourt, custom demanded we take tea in the studio where my father worked. He liked our being there. Our chitchat didn't disturb him at all. He went on working, facing the big bay window that looked out onto the garden, and there was something of the Sphinx in his mineral fixity.

I saw my father cry twice. The first time was when he informed us of Merleau-Ponty's death, the second when Caroline died. Struck head-on by a reckless Japanese driver on a seaside road at dusk, my sister died instantly. But the office colleague accompanying her "on assignment" to Juan-les-Pins said she cried out loudly just before the impact.

The coffin, brought to Paris by a small charter plane, was placed in the crypt of the church where the religious ceremony was to take place. My mother, pale and in shock, broke down over the coffin. My father arrived. They went to pick up the corpse. My "parents" ended up side by side. My father took my mother's hand, and tears clouded his face. In a way, she was *their* only child.

I have already mentioned my "illness" and certain of its symptoms. But that is not the point of my book. I will limit myself to mentioning only what is necessary to understand the things I have written here. The "hell" I spoke of lasted long past my return from the USSR. The idea of suicide began to haunt me as the only solution to my suffering. Hardly anything changed, despite my analysis. One night when I was at my father's "for an emergency," in despair, I raised a pressing question: What would become of me when he was no longer there to provide for me materially?

He looked at me with earnest compassion and told me tranquilly, as if it were a foregone conclusion: "But you will get *your share*."

The idea of inheritance, it seems, did not form part of my mental universe.

I saw my father for the last time—alive—nearly two years before his death. For a long time, I'd heard nothing from him. I was usually the one to call, to take the first step. At that time, I was testing him, and I kept my distance. I had stopped asking him for money to get by, and if I led an ascetic life in consequence, still, I was relieved at last to be making it on my own and to no longer have to "beg." There was no prior discussion: one day I just stopped going to get my "pension" in Gloria's back room. (Did my father realize this? Nothing indicates that he did. The only person who could have brought it to his attention was Gloria herself. Did she do so? I have no idea.)

Regardless, in March of 1980, I needed an operation and had no money for it and no insurance. Not without a certain malice (he doesn't care about me; fine, he'll have to now ...), I chose this occasion to see my father again. As usual, I made an appointment with Gloria. I entered the consulting room, where he waited for me, immobile, frozen, his face inscrutable, and asked him cheerfully what was new. He didn't respond, but instead asked me in a tone I'd never heard from him *what was it I wanted*. To talk, to see you ..., I said, stunned. But what else? Hurt, I replied that I needed an operation, that I didn't have the money to get it, and so I was hoping he would give it to me. His only response was *no*, then he got up to put an end to our "session." Not one single question about my health. Incredulous, I tried to "snap him out of it," but in vain, he just said *no* again and held the door open for me. My father had never treated me that way. For the first time, I had dealt with a stranger. On the sidewalk of Rue de Lille, I swore I would only see *that man* again on his deathbed.

It was only much later, too late, that Gloria told me that then—already—he had begun to tell everyone no. She had seen me leave distraught, I had told her all that had happened, why didn't she tell me at the time?

At the beginning of August 1981, Gloria—always Gloria—called me at home to recommend—but forcefully—I go visit my father in Guitrancourt. My father hadn't asked her to, but, she said, she was sure it would make him very happy. In essence, she was telling me it was my duty. Then she explained to me what had happened a year and a half before and revealed something I had no idea of: that my father was not well (oh, euphemism!). That was all it took, my resentment vanished, and I wanted to see him as soon as possible. Gloria, however—why?—set the appointment for the end of the month. Two or three weeks elapsed, and I eagerly prepared to see my father again. The night before our reunion, which, I remember clearly, was meant to take place on a Sunday, Gloria called again, this time to cancel. My father had to be hospitalized urgently "to run some tests." Where? There was no way of knowing. (My god! How "young" I was! How did I not demand she tell me where to find *my* father?) As far as the gravity of his situation, my father's secretary, now in the service, not of the Master, but of his daughter—the other one—would tell me nothing. Two weeks later, I left for Vienna, where I was employed for a stint as translator for an international organization.

On September 9, midafternoon, a phone call came to the office from my brother. My father was going to die that very night, he told me. I had to take the first plane back. As if you could catch a plane the same way you catch a taxi. I was in a suburb of Vienna and my passport and my things were in a hotel in the city. It was literally impossible to return to Paris that same day, and I had to settle for leaving the next morning. I was paralyzed. The death of one's father is inconceivable. Unable to be alone, I asked a colleague to dine with me and, after she left, I stayed behind drinking in the restaurant until late at night, one glass after the next.

Once in Paris, I called from the airport. My father *was no longer*. I went straight to Rue d'Assas, where Judith lived and where they had taken my father's body.

I accused my brother—who had gotten Gloria to tell him where my father was hospitalized and gone to his bedside every day, despite Judith's resistance—of concealing from me, *until the very last moment*, the certainty that he would die—the extreme gravity of the operation he'd undergone and of his state in general—death had been hovering over him the whole time—and of treating me, once more, like an inferior being. His explanation: he had asked my father every day if he wanted to see me, and my father—over and over—had answered *no*. But had my brother bothered to ask him if he wanted to see *him*?

I later learned that at the hospital, when the operation was over, my father was lucid again, albeit only for an instant, and remembered things as they'd been. I am sure that if I had been there, at one moment or another, he would have recognized me, and that the intervening years would have proven less painful for me.

My father's funeral was doubly sinister. First, I was burying my father, and naturally I would have liked the people who had cared for him to be there. Profiting from my stupor, from my brother's apathy, and from her privileged status, Judith opted, entirely on her own, for a "private" funeral for "intimate friends" and family, for that *funeral-abduction* which was announced in the press only after the fact and at which, moreover, I was subjected to the presence of all those little acolytes from the School of the Freudian Cause whose hands I refused to shake. Judith and Jacques-Alain Miller had organized everything. The whole clan was there, and Thibaut and I played the role of undesirables (only Marianne Merleau-Ponty came to embrace me). "Traitors, all of them," I thought.

The postmortem appropriation of Lacan, of *our* father, had begun. But how should a person react in the midst of mourning, forced to cope with calculating careerists? Everything happened too fast. Later, I would confront Judith—more and more, as the years passed—whenever I thought it necessary or permissible, but back then, my mind was elsewhere. The day after the funeral, I left for Vienna.

Several years after my father's death, I passed through Guitrancourt, where he is buried, on my way back from a weekend in Honfleur with my then-boyfriend. I no longer had my own car, and used the opportunity—a day away from Paris, a vehicle—to pay him a visit.

The cemetery at Guitrancourt is on a hillside at the edge of the village. Thankfully, the gate is always open, and you can enter without having to be let in. I asked my friend to wait for me on the road down below. I wanted to see my father alone, without witnesses, *one on one*. (We will overlook the young man's annoyed and sulky reaction.) It was to be a private, intimate engagement.

I walked through the rows of flower-bedecked graves (were the flowers artificial?) until I reached my father's, at the upper part of the enclosure. An ugly slab of cement with the traditional name and dates (birth, death). I was moved. It had been so many years since we'd talked.

The weather was fine and cool, the air bracing. I had brought a red rose with me. I placed it carefully on the headstone, looking a long time for the ideal position, then I stopped. I waited for contact to be established. Things were harder with the "idiot" waiting for me further down and distracting me with his ill humor. I tried in vain to concentrate, to be there completely.

As a last resort, I laid my hand on the icy stone until it burned. (How often, in the past, we had held each other's hand.) Reconciliation of bodies, reconciliation of souls. The magic worked. At last, I was with him. *Dear Papa, I love you. You are my father, you know.* He must have heard me.

Back in Paris, in the middle of the night, I wrote a long letter to a friend that ended, I remember, with the words: "We ought not to leave the dead too long alone."

Epilogue

THE "LAST DREAM"*

I dreamt my father was recovering (he hadn't died) and that we loved one another. Only he and I were really present. If others were around, they were mere bystanders, I didn't look at them, and they didn't intervene in any way.

It was a story of love, of passion. The risk still remained that he would die, because his "wound" could reopen at any moment and he wasn't careful. I was afraid, but there was nothing I could do.

*An excerpt from my diary, Vienna, September 19, 1981.
Dream noted down upon waking.

REQUIEM*

light. slight pounding of footsteps. among the group, children, flowers. the path rises softly toward the cemetery. the image both fixed and shifting. it is there that I cried: sealed in a coffin, death, now palpable, confronts color for the last time. mobile air, verdant horizons of hills, the trembling of the world.

*Excerpt from my diary, Paris, October 1981. The funeral: sketch.

In Élisabeth Roudinesco's *Jacques Lacan*, published in September 1993, the author describes, in the chapter "Tomb for a Pharaoh," my father's final moments.

She writes: "Abruptly, the sutures burst, provoking a peritonitis, followed by septicemia. The pain was atrocious. Like Max Schur at Freud's bedside, the doctor made the choice to administer the needed drug for a painless death. *At the last moment, Lacan looked daggers at him.*"*

When I read this last phrase, I was seized by an unutterable despair. I broke down in tears, which quickly turned into violent sobs. Flat on my stomach on the sofa in the "living room," I succumbed to a torrent of fiery tears that seemed as if they would never stop.

The idea that my father *saw* himself tumbling into nothingness, had known that in the next second *he would no longer be*, was unbearable. His fury at that instant, his refusal to accept the common lot of *all* men made him dearer to me, because I recognized him fully in it: "obstinate," to quote the last words attributed to him.

*My emphasis.

I believe that was the day I felt closest to my father. After that, I no longer cried when I thought of him.

August 1991–June 1994